Mel Bay Presents

JAZZ SOLOS FOR ACOUSTIC GUITAR

by Stanley Solow

Free audio available online!
Visit: www.melbay.com/93955

MEL BAY®

ISBN: 0-7866-0078-0

Visit us on the Web at www.melbay.com — E-mail us at email@melbay.com

ACKNOWLEDGEMENTS

To Guitarist August Lamont; the first to inform about Maestro Andres Segovia and his virtuoso multi-voice guitar performances.

To Joseph Barry Galbraith; Guitarist and mentor of note, responsible for the awakening of an entirely new plectrum guitar melodic and harmonic concept; and who suggested that I study classic guitar with:

(Prof.) Albert Valdes-Blain, student of Segovia who patiently explained the right hand classic technique, so that in time the great contrapuntal music of Milan, Dowland, Tarrega, Torroba, Hector-Villa Lobos, J. S. Bach, etc. could be admired, studied, analyzed and performed.

To William Irwin, keyboard artist; suggested that some original music be composed for guitar that would use scales, modes, harmonies and rhythms that could have only been derived from the great polyethnic society of the U.S.A.

To Mel Bay publishers for deeming this music worthy enough to publish.

For all the players; hopefully they will find these "Line On Line" compositions musical and technically challenging and that they be performed with a swinging elegance.

Stanley Solow, instructor of guitar at Hofstra University, Hempstead, N.Y. 1966–1986 and Nassau Community College, Garden City, N.Y. 1970 to the present.

A resident of New York City, where he attended Public School 44 (Bronx); Dewitt Clinton High School, and Columbia University. Served in U.S. Army 1942–45 with 445 AAA Bn., 8th Inf. Div.

Married to Rescue Lady Freda; two loving children, Paula Nan (Mrs. Bruce) Watkins, and French hornist Harold Tobias, and their families.

Compact disc recorded by Raymond Penney.

Explanation of terms and symbols used in this book.

RIGHT HAND

> P = *Thumb*
> i = *Index*
> m = *Middle*
> a = *Ring*

LEFT HAND

1, 2, 3, 4
O = *open string*

TABLATURE EXPLAINED

Circle = String
Uncircled = Fret

Number in Circle = String
C = Capodastro (Barre)   Roman Numerals = Position
"Blues as Blues is" Chord with arrow attached to 'a'. Play chord as shown then 'arpeggiate' chord with ring finger from highest note to low 'd' in bass.

D.S. (del segno) = return to sign
al fine = play until 'fine' (end)

H = Harmonics. Touch string with index finger 12 frets higher than note depressed with left finger. Pluck with 'a'.

D.C. (da capo) = return to beginning; play until sign
Golpe = Strike saddle bone with right thumb.
Staccato = lift left fingers immediately after striking note
Rasgueado = A nail scratch. Hold chord with left fingers and cascade the fingers of the right hand in the following order: little, ring, middle, index.

Micro = 'bend' string with left finger until microtone is heard.
Tambour = Strike saddle bone gently with palm of the left hand causing strings to vibrate.
Pizzicatto = Rest heel of right hand on strings at saddle bone; pluck with right thumb.

6 = D Tune Harmonic 12 fret 6 string to open 4 string.

⌇ = descending mordent; written note plus note below (in key), then back to original note, played very rapidly.

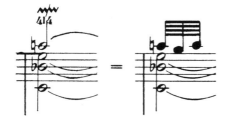

⌇ = mordent; written note plus note above then back to original note.

Instructions for tablature players: All terms and symbols used in this book appear in the notation section, above the tablature.

VOUS TUTTIS VEIGH

S. SOLOW

Guitar

SUSAN J.

Guitar

S. SOLOW

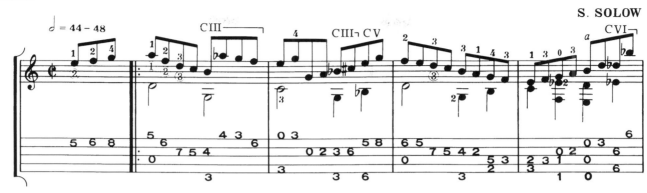

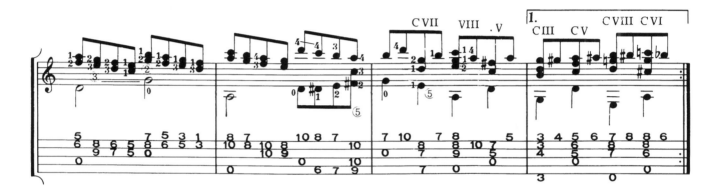

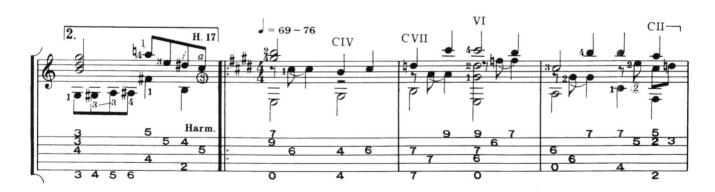

BLUES AS BLUES IS

Guitar

S. SOLOW

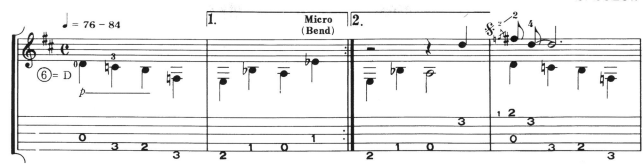

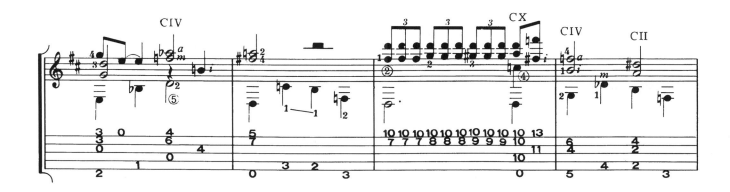

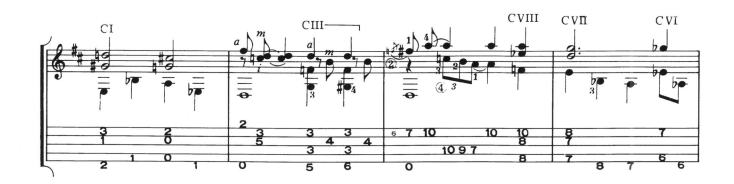

LITTLE ROBERT

Guitar

S. SOLOW

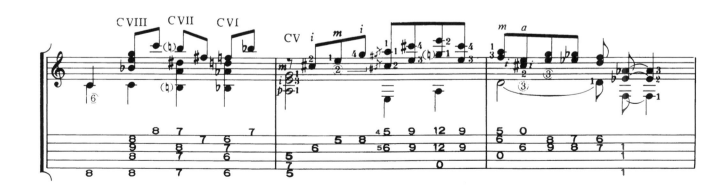

BLUES FOR MONDAY

Guitar

S. SOLOW

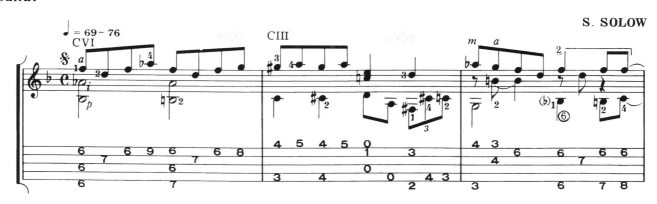

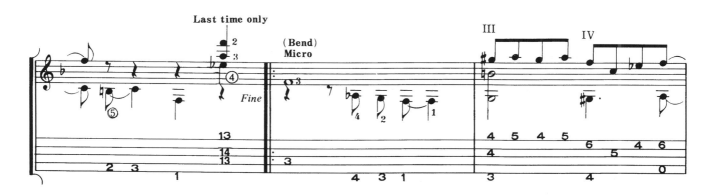

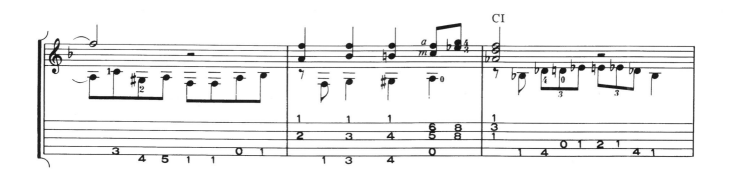

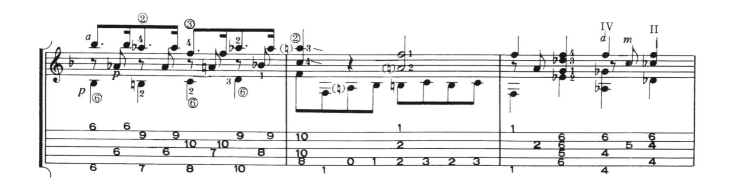

TAPESTRY

Guitar

By: S. Solow

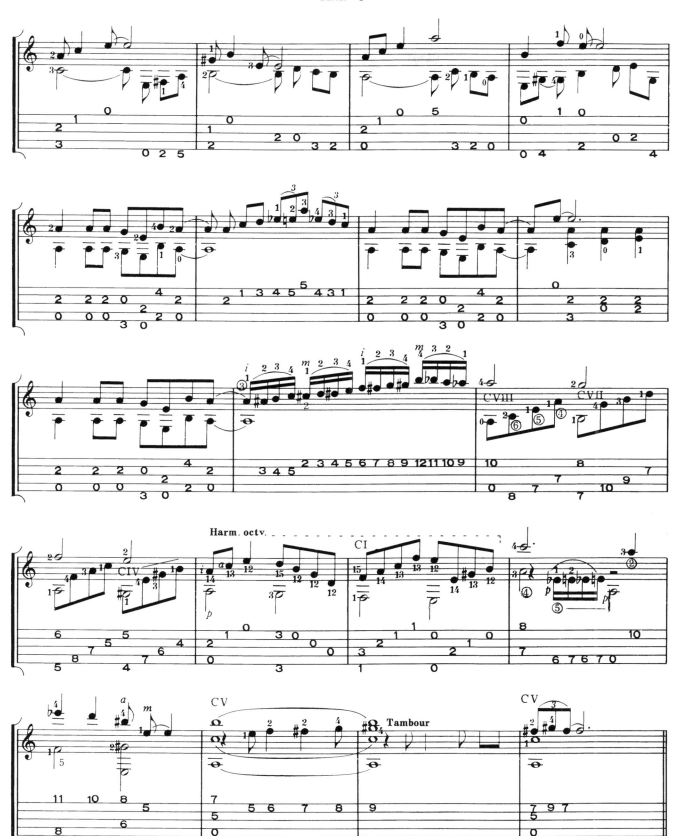

OPUS UNTITLED

Guitar

By: S. Solow

SWORDS INTO PLOWSHARES

Guitar

S. SOLOW

FREDA TO THE RESCUE

Guitar

S. SOLOW

A * B * C *

Guitar

S. SOLOW

THEME AND VARIATION IN "A" MAJOR

"In Memory of Louis Sosa: A Great Guitarist"

Guitar

By: S. Solow

25

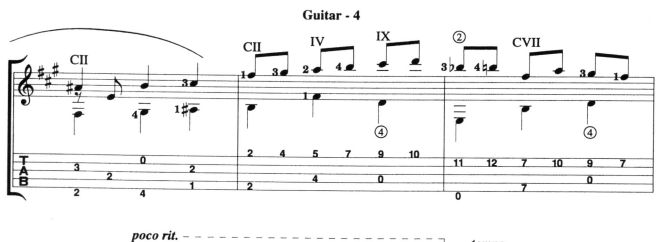

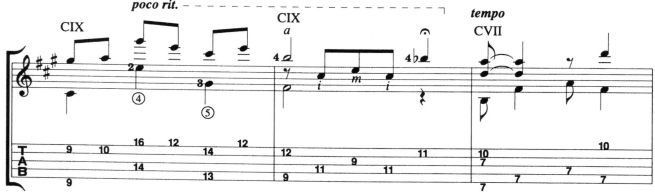

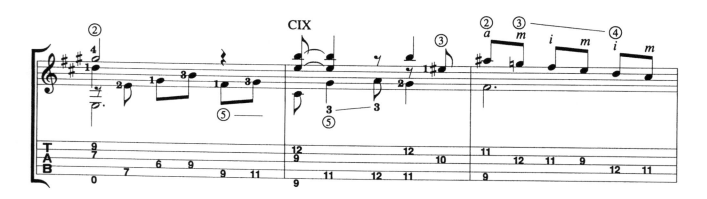

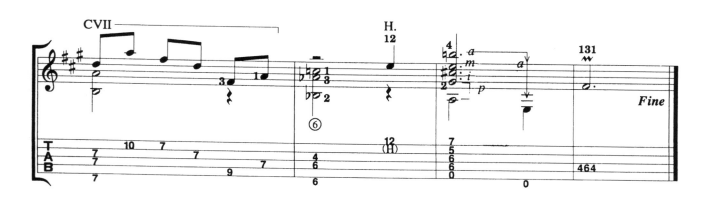

LONG ISLAND EXPRESSWAY BLUES, EAST & WEST

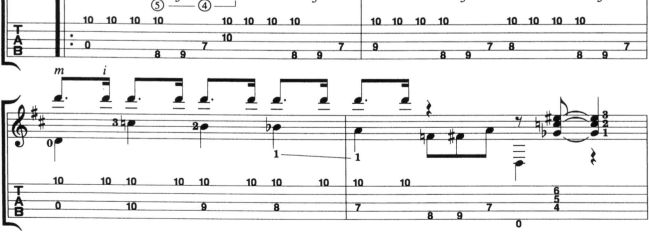

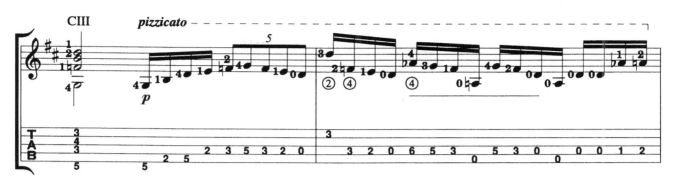

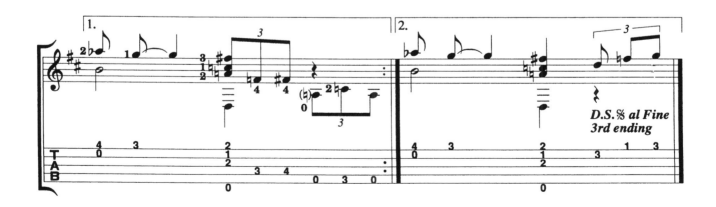

Printed in Great Britain
by Amazon